Follow Me - A Seasonal Journey

by Lana Lee Marler

A Personal Worship Resource for the Church Calendar Year
(Includes Journal with Audio Narration and Music)

Featuring the Paintings of Daniel Bonnell
with
Reflections from Contributing Writer, Roger Housden

Book Cover Art: The Baptism of the Christ #2 by Daniel Bonnell
Title Page Art: *The Pearl of Great Price* by Daniel Bonnell

WestBow Press books may be ordered through booksellers or by contacting:

WestBow Press
A Division of Thomas Nelson & Zondervan
1663 Liberty Drive
Bloomington, IN 47403
www.westbowpress.com
1 (866) 928-1240

ISBN: 978-1-5127-9180-8 (sc)
ISBN: 978-1-5127-9181-5 (e)

Library of Congress Control Number: 2017909616

Printed in China.

WestBow Press rev. date: 10/20/2017

WESTBOW
P R E S S®
A DIVISION OF THOMAS NELSON
& ZONDERVAN

In Dedication

To Frances and Harry, my mother and father,
for their steadfast love and forbearance, serving as
standard-bearers for excellence before their children;

To Bill, my husband-friend, teacher and encourager;

and

To Jacob, my son and only child,
whose gift has been to open my eyes and heart to the
unconditional Love of God.

A Word of Special Thanks

to

Daniel Bonnell
and
Roger Housden

for

Generosity of Spirit and Collaboration
in this Labor of Love

In Gratitude

To Dr. Robert G. Lee, my namesake and childhood pastor,
For leading me to faith in Christ and believer's baptism;
Thank you for the image I have of you
kneeling beside the pulpit each Sunday morning
in prayer and humility before you preached.

To The Rev. L. Noland Pipes, Jr.,
Pastor, Priest and Mentor in my adult faith journey;
You have been a *Father* to me in the church and like my *father*
since my earthly father went to heaven.
Thank you for teaching me faithfulness
and how to encourage others.

To The Rev. Andy Andrews,
Priest, Friend and Brother in Christ
Thank you for being a living example of *The Good Shepherd* and
for consistently holding-up God's mirror revealing that
I am beautiful and beloved of my Maker.

Contents

* Chapter Title Pages Abstract Cross Art: *Untitled* by Mike Irwin

Music Only Download Link

http://jacobsladdercdc.org/follow_me_a_seasonal_journey_music.zip

Narration with Music Download Link

http://jacobsladdercdc.org/follow_me_a_seasonal_journey_audio_narration.zip

Foreword

As I first read this salute to the spiritual journey to which we are all called, a phrase that is special to me kept running through my mind. I had come to love the term, *well-tuned heart*, which I discovered in a verse from the hymn, "Ye Holy Angels Bright." The words originated with Richard Baxter (1615-1691) as follows: *My soul, bear thou thy part, triumph in God above: and with a well-tuned heart sing thou the songs of love! Let all thy days till life shall end, what e'er he send be filled with praise.*

And then, later on in my own journey, I was delighted to discover a similar reference in Robert Robinson's "Come thou fount of every blessing, tune my heart to sing thy grace!" The well-tuned heart is required of us if we are to give God the praise He desires and for which we were created. As you read and live with the words which follow in this book and the music which accompanies them, I trust that you, too, will enjoy the experience of a well-turned heart.

Lana Marler has been a friend and a blessing for some twenty years. Her well-tuned heart became obvious early on and I trust that you, dear reader, will be equally blessed by that which Lana offers from her heart. Hers is a fruitful invitation to follow the paths of the Christian organization of the yearly calendar that will surely tune one's heart.

The origins of this ancient process by which Christians have long-practiced the sanctification of time have been lost to my memory. It is enough to know that our spiritual ancestors, Jew and Gentile, learned and practiced the recognition of God's presence and activity in their lives by consolidating periods of time with particular events and memories. So it is for those of us in our own time, as we move from season to season on our spiritual journeys.

The benefits of this journey are important. First, we are protected from ourselves... from the tendency to prefer particular parts and passages from Holy Scripture. The seasons invite us to disciplined reflection and repentance as much as to unrestrained joy and celebration. In the process, we are led through a far more comprehensive exposure to God's self disclosure than would be likely if left to our own devices. Secondly, our attention is focused on the essence of God's revelation and we are led step-by-step to the origins of the creeds and statements of belief we often rehearse.

In short, this is an invitation to the *tuning of your heart*. Read and sing with Lana and be richly blessed.

The Rev. L. Noland Pipes, Jr.

Preface

I lived with my parents on a twenty-acre farm outside of Memphis, Tennessee for the first four years of my life. My father was a businessman and made his living in the city but he also raised white-faced herefords on that small piece of real estate we enjoyed as our "heaven on earth." We had other animals on the farm as well - a horse, 2 hunting dogs, a dozen or so puppies and a white pet duck I named Liberace. I loved all the animals and was comforted by the energetic life of each as well as their abiding presence which offered a daily peace to our lives. But even as a young child, I was not able to fully embrace the peace afforded to me by my circumstances. I did not want to be away from my mother's side and clung to her to the point that many times she could not go about her chores.

One of the earliest formative experiences from my childhood is not only indelible in my memory but would be a predictive pattern for my life thereafter. I had been admonished by my mother to stay outside and play for a while so that she could get some work done, but the swing set in the fenced play area outside the farmhouse brought no new challenges and I had become bored. I kept coming in and out of the house, plaguing my mother with questions and entreaties, until finally, upon leaving the house for the last time, the door shut behind me and I was not able to open it again. With my father working in the city and having no siblings at that time, my mother was the center of my world and the source of love and security on which I depended. I remember feeling panic to be separated from her, so in my desperation, I found a vent in the foundation of the farmhouse and crawled through the menacing dark space, emerging from the other side only a few feet from the back kitchen door which I burst through like a drowning person coming up for air.

Over the years the same scenario of my desperate crawl to gain entrance into that place of love and acceptance played-out more times than one could count. It would be much later when I would realize as an adult that my desperation for the peace and security represented by my mother's love and presence mirrored my soul's need for God. Not until

I embraced the source of that need did I begin to develop a wider perspective on life and my place in God's creation. No longer could my soul's hunger be satisfied with anything less than a close relationship with the "Lover of my soul" as revealed in the person of Jesus Christ.

Lana Lee Marler

Introduction

C. S. Lewis, the 20th century Anglican author, notes in his writings that **people like variety but they also like things to stay the same**. The yearly remembrance of the sacred seasons of the Church and expository biblical texts satisfies the human need for *that which changes and that which changes not*. Suitably designed, the Liturgical Calendar is a gift which the Church gives to itself - a familiar and well-worn path traversed by countless pilgrims on their journey toward the Light of God. Just as yearly calendars mark the passing of time and changes in the seasons, the yearly calendar of the Western Church (which includes both Protestant and Catholic traditions) highlights the life and ministry of Jesus as it moves through the changing seasons. The observance of the various seasons in the Church year includes particular events, holidays and festivals deemed sacred and central to the faith of those following *the way of Christ*, and offers its disciples opportunities for education and spiritual growth. Consequently, worshipers are presented, in an organized fashion, with occasions to recall the life of Christ by journeying with Him. From His promised coming at Advent, His earthly life and ministry, His death, burial and Resurrection, to the birth of the Church at Pentecost and His promised return at Advent II, congregations trod the path with Jesus and re-live His life. It is here that wayfaring strangers are strangers no more and the Church begins to look and behave like the *Bride of Christ* because they have entered into a dialogue regarding their own faith journey each calendar year.

Following His baptism and temptation in the wilderness, Jesus began His three-year public ministry on the earth. To His disciples, the rich young ruler and sincere seekers after truth and the path to eternal life, Jesus consistently responded with these words: "Follow Me." It is Christ's call to discipleship for me which was the motivation for the personal worship resource and journal presented here. When I first embraced the Lord as the "Lover of my soul," I did not comprehend the nature and depth of that love. The unveiling of the risen Christ to my soul was to be a gradual process which still continues to unfold as *I see through a glass darkly*, longing to *see face to face*. (I Cor. 13:12a KJV)

We know that the followers of Christ who did see Him face to face made special note of the extraordinary events they observed and experienced through the Gospel accounts of the New Testament. As sensory beings, eye-witnesses heard the angels sing at Jesus' birth, listened to His preaching by the seashore and on the hillsides around Jerusalem as well as the cries from the roaring crowds clamoring for his crucifixion; they sniffed the sweet fragrance of hay, the dust and dung of animals present at the manger, and the smell of fear which engulfed the disillusioned disciples scattering at His death; they touched the hem of His garment in faith, his feet in worship and in fear and doubt, touched the palms of His hands which bore the nail scars; they tasted His *new* wine at a marriage feast and fish He cooked for them over an open fire at the seashore, as well as the broken bread and wine at the Last Supper; they saw Him feed the multitudes, heal lepers, and comfort His mother. Eye-witnesses saw Him offer Himself for torture and death on a cross, be resurrected from the dead after three days and then ascend through the skies back to the heavenly Father.

Because a purposeful observance of the various seasons of the Church calendar involves all the senses, this book offers to the follower of Christ opportunities to experience scripture, teachings, art, poetry, and music centered around the Liturgical calendar and then reflect on these experiences by keeping a three-year journal. In *Prayers of Life,* Michel Quoist put it this way:

> *The Father has put us into the world, not to walk through it with lowered eyes, but to search for Him through things, events, people. Everything must reveal God to us.*

Utilizing this personal worship resource, you are invited to search for and experience the *God Who is with us* - visually, auditorily, and tactilely. Please Note: If you journal by the light of a fragrant candle while sipping a cup of coffee or a glass of wine, all the senses will be involved.

Lana Lee Marler

The
Season
of
Advent

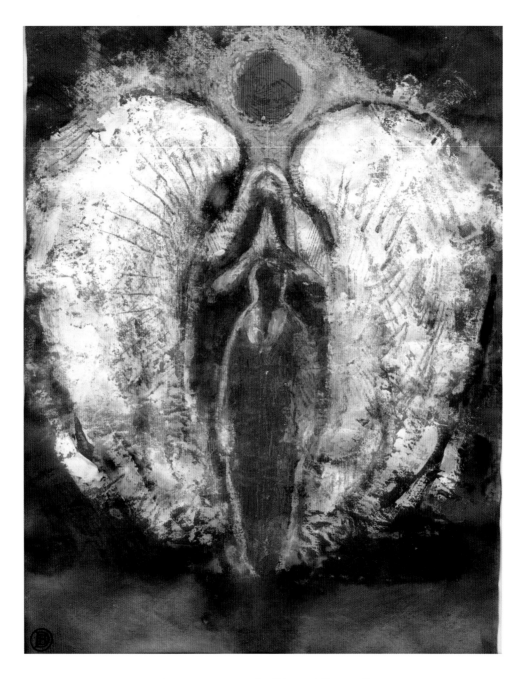

Annunciation #3 by Daniel Bonnell

Advent

"God sent the angel Gabriel to Nazareth, a town in Galilee, to a virgin pledged to be married to a man named Joseph, a descendant of David. The virgin's name was Mary. The angel went to her and said, "Greetings, you who are highly favored! The Lord is with you." Mary was greatly troubled at his words and wondered what kind of greeting this might be. But the angel said to her, "Do not be afraid, Mary; you have found favor with God. You will conceive and give birth to a son, and you are to call him Jesus. He will be great and will be called the Son of the Most High. The Lord God will give him the throne of his father David, and He will reign over Jacob's descendants forever; His kingdom will never end." "How will this be," Mary asked the angel, "since I am a virgin?" The angel answered, "The Holy Spirit will come on you, and the power of the Most High will overshadow you. So the holy one to be born will be called the Son of God."

Luke 1:26-35 NIV

Advent is the beginning of the Church Year for most churches in the tradition of Western Christianity. It begins on the fourth Sunday before Christmas Day, which is the Sunday nearest to November 30, and ends on Christmas Eve (Dec. 24). The traditional color used for clergy vestments and hangings to adorn the Sanctuary during Advent is purple. (In recent years, however, there has been an increasing practice of replacing purple with blue in the Advent Season to denote a hopeful attitude of awe and anticipation, because the color purple is so readily identified with the penitential character of the Lenten Season.) Advent, meaning "coming" or "arrival," is a season for spiritual preparation for the birth of Christ coming into the world to dispel the darkness of sin. This time is characterized by the tensions of opposites: darkness and light, fear and hope, self-centeredness and self-sacrifice, discomfort and deliverance, as we, the Church, make our own pilgrimage to Bethlehem with the Holy Family. As a people who walk in darkness, doubt, and fear, we hope for the light and reconciliation with God. Each Sunday of Advent brings us closer to the appointed time and candles are lit in anticipation. Prayer, reflection, expectation, and longing mark this season for us, as it did for the Virgin Mary, and we are comforted that, if we prepare a place in our hearts for the Messiah, He will share the journey with us.

Head of Mary by Daniel Bonnell

The Longing

by

Lana Lee Marler

When will it stop - the pain of this longing?
Seeming without beginning or ending.
Standing or sitting, lying or sleeping;
This ever-present longing.

Inside and out, my soul's tears are falling.
It's me and not - close but far - this longing.
Glimpsing does not permit the heart's holding;
Nor a brushed cheek soothed from aching.

All those who do not know this longing,
Pity me not, my life thus disgracing;
For this poor heart would spend itself wandering
Down paths sure to find it embracing.

What kind of peace inhabits this longing?
Husbanded by great toil and striving.
Not an easy peace won in the struggling,
But peace without which there's no living.

All those who do not know this longing,
Pity me not, my life thus disgracing;
For this poor heart would spend itself wandering
Down paths sure to find it embracing.

Therefore I'll cling to this blanket of longing,
So long as my heart beats 'neath its swaddling.
Where it takes me is not for the caring;
Just to know and be known...The journey sharing.

Reflection on "The Longing"
by Roger Housden

What is this longing for something we cannot quite name which for so many seems to accompany all of their days? Poets of all cultures have spoken of it for centuries, as if it naturally draws forth our aspiration for a life more complete and whole than the one we presently know. Yet, at the same time, this new life is not separate from who and where we are now. It seems to be as close as the air we breathe, and this is why Advent is the perfect time for us to feel and celebrate this longing inside us for what is beyond all words. Mary is with child; she contains a mystery that has still to emerge into the light of day, and yet the presence of which colors all of her days. She knows she is giving birth to a new reality, but does not yet know quite what that means. There is a sweet pain to pregnancy, which this poem refers to in its first line. Rumi captures the paradox in these lines of one of his poems:

Listen to the moan of a dog for its master.
That whining is the connection.

Reflect on your own experience of longing. Follow it down to its source, not so much by thinking about it but by feeling the sensations of it in your body. Bring your attention to your chest area. Let yourself abide there in a wordless gesture of bowing to the mystery of your own life. Write a few lines on your experience of this.

Advent | Reflections 20__

Advent | Reflections 20___

Advent | Reflections 20__

Advent | Reflections 20___

Advent | Reflections 20__

Advent | Reflections 20__

Advent | Reflections 20__

Advent | Reflections 20___

Advent | Reflections 20__

The
Season
of
Christmas

Seeing Shepherds by Daniel Bonnell

Christmas

"In those days Caesar Augustus issued a decree that a census should be taken of the entire Roman world. (This was the first census that took place while Quirinius was governor of Syria.) And everyone went to their own town to register. So Joseph also went up from the town of Nazareth in Galilee to Judea, to Bethlehem the town of David, because he belonged to the house and line of David. He went there to register with Mary, who was pledged to be married to him and was expecting a child. While they were there, the time came for the baby to be born, and she gave birth to her firstborn, a son. She wrapped him in cloths and placed him in a manger, because there was no guest room available for them. And there were shepherds living out in the fields nearby, keeping watch over their flocks at night. An angel of the Lord appeared to them, and the glory of the Lord shone around them, and they were terrified. But the angel said to them, 'Do not be afraid, I bring you good news that will cause great joy for all the people. Today in the town of David a Savior has been born to you; he is the Messiah, the Lord. This will be a sign to you: You will find a baby wrapped in cloths and lying in a manger.' Suddenly a great company of the heavenly host appeared with the angel, praising God and saying, 'Glory to God in the highest heaven, and on earth peace to those on whom his favor rests.' When the angels had left them and gone into heaven, the shepherds said to one another, 'Let's go to Bethlehem and see this thing that has happened, which the Lord has told us about.' So they hurried off and found Mary and Joseph, and the baby, who was lying in the manger. When they had seen him, they spread the word concerning what had been told them about this child, and all who heard it were amazed at what the shepherds said to them. But Mary treasured up all these things and pondered them in her heart. The shepherds returned, glorifying and praising God for all the things they had heard and seen, which were just as they had been told." Luke 2:1-20 NIV

Each year on Christmas Day, the liturgical color for Sanctuary adornments changes from purple or blue to white - the color which symbolizes purity and reverence, used for all High Holy Days and festival days of the Church Year. But in traditional Christian churches, the commemoration of the birth of Christ is not just one High and Holy Day, but a seasonal celebration lasting twelve days in the church calendar. Most historians agree that by the early fourth century Christians began celebrating the birth of Jesus as an alternative to the pagan celebration of the birth of the sun at the winter solstice on Dec. 25, which heralded the onset of spring and renewal on the earth after the long travail of winter. The nativity story in Luke's gospel is told from Mary's perspective as she endures a season of labor, *before* the fact, to reconcile the conflict of her thoughts and emotions regarding this extraordinary event. Having found favor with God, Mary is to become the *Theotokos - Mother of The Most High God*. Troubled and afraid, she feels unequal to the task as an earthen vessel to carry the "Holy Other" in her body, but nevertheless submits herself to the will of God. From this point, Christ was born into this world in silent isolation as a gradual manifestation in Mary's own heart as well as her body.

Mary and Her Baby by Daniel Bonnell

24

Even So, Come
by
Lana Lee Marler

Come, Lord Jesus; Come, Lord Jesus.
In the hush of the trembling stillness,
So silent are your gentle stirrings
On the scattered straw.

O Come, Lord Jesus; Come, Lord Jesus.
In this moment, scarcely can I breathe,
So sweet is Your breath born
In the stable of this poor heart.

Even so, Come.

Reflection on "Even So, Come"
by Roger Housden

This poem captures perfectly the moment that the longing is responded to and a new life is born from the old. The stirrings of a new life are silent and gentle, and care and attention is needed to hear them. But when you do, they are unmistakable, and you know it is time to bring forth what you may have sensed all along but not had the capacity to bring into form. Notice that the poet says,

Your breath is born in the stable of this poor heart,

- poor, because the heart must be emptied of self, of our familiar identity, for a new life to come forth. "Poor" implies humility, self-emptying.

Have you known a moment or time when your familiar identity was forgotten and you experienced yourself anew in some way?

Describe this experience.

Christmas Reflections 20___

Christmas Reflections 20__

Christmas Reflections 20__

Christmas Reflections 20__

Christmas Reflections 20__

Christmas Reflections 20__

Christmas Reflections 20__

Christmas Reflections 20__

Christmas Reflections 20___

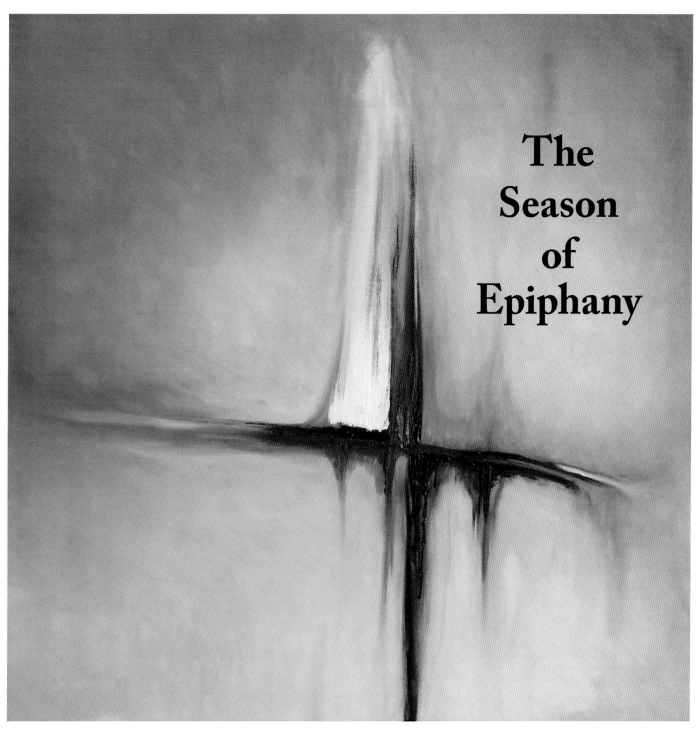

The
Season
of
Epiphany

Three Wise Men by Roy Borrone

38

Epiphany

"When Jesus was born in Bethlehem of Judea, in the days of King Herod, behold, magi from the east arrived in Jerusalem, saying, "Where is the newborn king of the Jews? We saw his star at its rising and have come to do him homage." When King Herod heard this, he was greatly troubled, and all Jerusalem with him. Assembling all the chief priests and the scribes of the people, He inquired of them where the Christ was to be born. They said to him, "In Bethlehem of Judea, for thus it has been written through the prophet: *And you, Bethlehem, land of Judah, are by no means least among the rulers of Judah; since from you shall come a ruler, who is to shepherd my people Israel.*" Then Herod called the magi secretly and ascertained from them the time of the star's appearance. He sent them to Bethlehem and said, "Go and search diligently for the child. When you have found him, bring me word, that I too may go and do him homage." After their audience with the king they set out. And behold, the star that they had seen at its rising preceded them, until it came and stopped over the place where the child was. They were overjoyed at seeing the star, and on entering the house they saw the child with Mary his mother. They prostrated themselves and did him homage. Then they opened their treasures and offered him gifts of gold, frankincense, and myrrh. And having been warned in a dream not to return to Herod, they departed for their country by another way." Matt. 2:1-12 KJV

Epiphany is celebrated on Jan. 6 and marks the climax of the Advent and Christmas Seasons. It is celebrated as a season of the church year for many Protestant traditions, extending until the beginning of Lent on Ash Wednesday, which, depending on the timing of Easter, could be four to nine Sundays. The Roman Catholic tradition observes Epiphany on Jan. 6, *only*, with the Sundays following referred to as *Ordinary Time*. The traditional color used for Sanctuary adornments during the Epiphany Season is white and changes to green on the Sundays which follow until Ash Wednesday. Epiphany means *manifestation, appearance...revelation* or *a new way of thinking*. Liturgically, the *Epiphany* commemorates the visitation of the Wise Men or Magi to the Christ-child. As astrologers, they had long-searched the night sky for a sign to indicate where the Promised Messiah would be born. Then after two years and a 600 mile journey, they found the toddler Jesus, gave to Him costly gifts of gold, frankincense and myrrh and bowed down to worship Him as King, thus revealing Jesus to be God Incarnate and Savior of all mankind. In tradition, these first Gentile seekers of truth and followers of Christ, are called Wise Men - a title more costly than the gifts they bestowed on their King. Searching the night sky for a sign - any sign, no matter how indistinct - presupposes a search in the night of the soul. One can only encounter the light of the Living God after having become exhausted and despairing from staring into the dark recesses of one's self.

Resurrection #2 by Daniel Bonnell

Epiphany
by
Lana Lee Marler

Peering...pathless...
Lidless eyes searching the night of self.
Leering...jeering...
Lying eyes shunning the bright darkness.
Blinded, bound and gagging...gazing;
Hoping...hopeless...the gaze...met;
And longing...longed-for...
The lamps of the soul... lit.

Reflection on "Epiphany"
by Roger Housden

All the characters in the passion play of Christ live within us. They all represent different stages of the journey of the human soul, as well as the intrinsic divinity of every individual which is pointed to in the common phrase, "Christ in you." Epiphany symbolizes that time when we are looking everywhere for some sign of the great beauty we know is so close and yet we cannot as yet see. The place where we need to look most deeply is in the night of our own self, because there, in the darkest night, is where the star we are looking for can appear. The poet Theodore Roethke said:

In a dark time, the eyes begin to see.

Have you known a time of darkness - of unknowing and perplexity - out of which new life has sprung?

What was the star you followed that led you out of the dark?

Epiphany Reflections 20__

Epiphany Reflections 20__

Epiphany Reflections 20___

Epiphany Reflections 20__

Epiphany Reflections 20___

Epiphany Reflections 20__

Epiphany Reflections 20__

Epiphany Reflections 20__

Epiphany Reflections 20__

The
Season
of
Lent

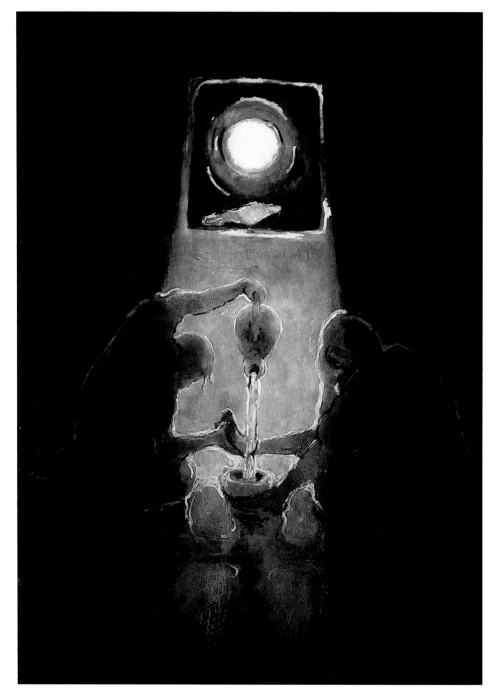

Footwasher by Daniel Bonnell

56

Lent

"Have mercy on me, O God, according to your unfailing love; according to your great compassion blot out my transgressions. Wash away all my iniquity and cleanse me from my sin. For I know my transgressions, and my sin is always before me. Against you, you only, have I sinned and done what is evil in your sight; so you are right in your verdict and justified when you judge. Surely I was sinful at birth, sinful from the time my mother conceived me. Yet you desired faithfulness even in the womb; you taught me wisdom in that secret place. Cleanse me with hyssop, and I will be clean; wash me, and I will be whiter than snow. Let me hear joy and gladness; let the bones you have crushed rejoice. Hide your face from my sins and blot out all my iniquity. Create in me a pure heart, O God, and renew a steadfast spirit within me. Do not cast me from your presence or take your Holy Spirit from me." Psalm 51:1-11 NIV

The word Lent was derived from the Old English word, *lenctentid*, meaning the time of lengthening, when the days begin to grow longer in the Spring. It was also the word for "March," the month in which the majority of Lent falls. The Lenten Season lasts for 40 days, not including Sundays, beginning on the seventh Wednesday before Easter Sunday (Ash Wednesday), and ends on the Saturday before Easter. Ash Wednesday originated in the early church ritual of imposing ashes on worshipers' foreheads as a sign of mortality and repentance before God. The liturgical color used for clergy vestments and hangings to adorn the Sanctuary for the Season of Lent is purple - the color of royalty...the color of the robe Pilate placed on Jesus. Hence, the color purple can also symbolize not only the pain and suffering of Jesus, but our subsequent mourning and penitence. The Season of Lent began to be observed in the fourth century as a time for fasting, penitential prayer, sacrifice and good works as a preparation of converts for baptism at Easter. It was also a time for those who had been separated from God and the church because of sin, to prepare to join the fellowship once more and then finally, Lent came to be observed as a season of penance for all Christians. It focuses attention on the need to die to oneself, turn from sin, and alter the direction of our lives in submission to the will of God. In so doing, the way is open for Christians to journey with Christ toward His cross of suffering in a spiritual pilgrimage through darkness and death as a means of our own spiritual renewal at His resurrection.

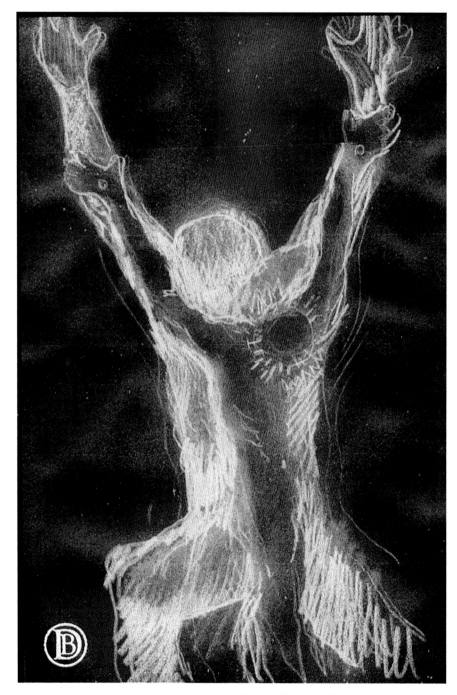

Resurrection #3 by Daniel Bonnell

Surrender

by
Lana Lee Marler

There is a point beneath the wake
When all the senses blur;
Where sight and sound and life's dull ache
Sink past all things that were.
Pressing desires and thoughts grown still
As once upon a dream,
Drift now so gently on the Will
Of the Maker of the stream.

What grand design has brought me thus,
So poised in space and time?
With outstretched arms as on a cross,
My life will soon be Thine.
O God, my heart cries out to You.
Leave not my soul in death;
But raise me up to life anew,
Filled with Your Holy Breath.

Reflection on "Surrender"
by Roger Housden

What is it we are called to surrender to the Maker of the stream? Lent is a time of chastening, a wonderful old English word which, rather than its more recent connotation of punishment, meant to refine or purify - "to make straight". What Lent encourages us to purify - to let go of - is our idea of who we think we are - a separate individual who thinks he is in control of his life - and to bow to our greater identity, which is the boundless and ineffable spirit who is the Maker of the Stream. The outer sacrifice of certain habits and foods at this time is a way of giving form and substance to the deeper sacrifice of our solid sense of identity, and to opening the door of the heart to the larger life that awaits us all.

When you read the word 'surrender', what thoughts and feelings come into your mind? What do you feel you need to let go of in order to enter a deeper, more soulful life?

Lenten Reflections 20__

Lenten Reflections 20__

Lenten Reflections 20___

Lenten Reflections 20__

Lenten Reflections 20__

Lenten Reflections 20___

Lenten Reflections 20__

Lenten Reflections 20___

Lenten Reflections 20___

The
Season
of
Easter

The Upside Down Sunset
by Daniel Bonnell

Road to Emmaus #2
by Daniel Bonnell

Easter

"But on the first day of the week, at early dawn, they went to the tomb, taking the spices which they had prepared. And they found the stone rolled away from the tomb, but when they went in they did not find the body. While they were perplexed about this, behold, two men stood by them in dazzling apparel; and as they were frightened and bowed their faces to the ground, the men said to them, "Why do you seek the living among the dead? Remember how he told you, while he was still in Galilee, that the Son of man must be delivered into the hands of sinful men, and be crucified, and on the third day rise." And they remembered his words, and returning from the tomb they told all this to the eleven and to all the rest." Luke 24:1-11 NRSV

Lasting fifty days and central to the entire Liturgical calendar, Easter or Eastertide is the climax of Lent and most sacred of all Seasons in the church year. The color white - the symbolic color for purity - is used for Sanctuary adornments during the Easter Season. Christians have observed Easter as the annual celebration of the Resurrection of Christ from the dead since the fourth century. Each year Easter falls on the first Sunday after the full moon following the Spring Equinox (March 21), so depending on the lunar cycle, the date of Easter can fluctuate between March 22 and April 25. The sixth week of Lent just preceding Easter is known as "Holy Week," wherein the events leading to the death, burial, and resurrection of Jesus are commemorated. It begins on Palm Sunday when the messianic entry of Christ as King into Jerusalem is celebrated with joyful "Hosannas" and the waving of palm branches. This Sunday is also known as Passion Sunday because it speaks to Jesus' proclamation of His impending Passion. The shadows of darkness, betrayal, suffering and death permeate the Holy Week observances, particularly "Good Friday" (formerly known as God's Friday) or "Holy Friday," the day of Christ's redemptive death as foretold by the prophet Isaiah: *He (Christ) had no dignity or beauty to make us take notice of Him. There was nothing attractive about him, nothing that would draw us to Him. We despised Him and rejected Him; He endured suffering and pain. No one would even look at Him - we ignored Him as if He were nothing. But He endured the suffering that should have been ours. Isaiah 53:2b-4 GNT*

Only in the shadow of the Cross of the Suffering Christ, "in Whom God was reconciling the world to Himself" (II Cor. 5:19 NEB), can the brightness and glory of His Easter Resurrection be truly experienced. The ecstatic ringing of bells and "Alleluias" sung by the faithful during this most joyful time of the year, bears witness to the world that through Christ's Resurrection from the grave, there is eternal salvation and hope for those that believe in Him. In many churches on Easter Sunday, the Cross casts a different shadow through a tradition known as "The Flowering of the Cross." Beautiful flowers are placed on the cross to signify that sins which had been nailed there have now been transformed by the sacrificial love of Christ and mankind is forever drawn to the beauty of that love.

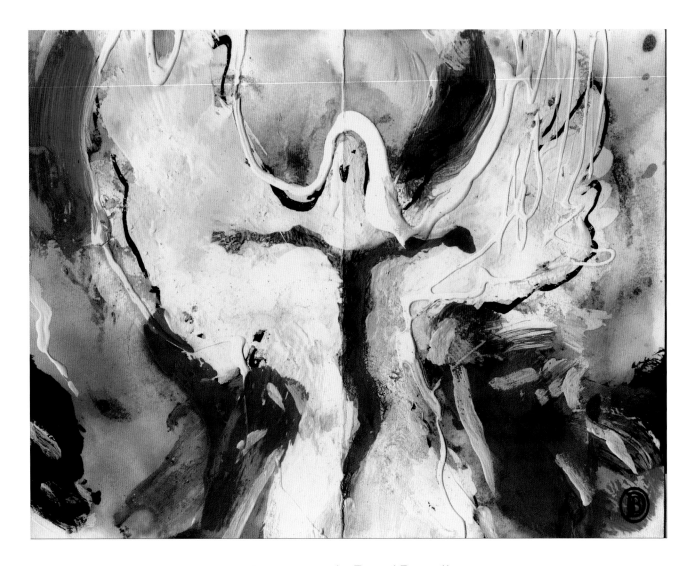

Christ Flight 2 by Daniel Bonnell

The Beauty of Your Love
by
Lana Lee Marler

O Lamb of God, the beauty of Your Love;
Flows through all time and space from above.
But, all the while, my soul knew not its name;
'Til I beheld Your Cross of sin and shame.

O Christ, my Savior, seems as if I see;
A thorny crown, Your head weighed down.
How can this be, such perfect love for me
Bore all my guilt by hanging on a tree?

O Lamb of God, Love shines from heaven's shore;
My risen Lord, alive forevermore.
No tomb can hold - "O Death, where is thy sting?"
Throughout the ages, I will ever sing -

What wondrous Love is this, O my soul!

Reflection on "The Beauty of Your Love"
by Roger Housden

There is a way of seeing that can acknowledge the special beauty that exists even in the midst of the pain of darkness. This kind of beauty is everlasting. It cannot be touched by decay or death. It is the beauty that emerges from the supreme sacrifice of our human self to the one Self we call God. This is Christ's resurrection. It can appear to our eyes as a miracle, because it does not abide by the laws of our familiar world. Yet though its source is from elsewhere, its light and beauty permeates this world as well as the next - again, for those that have eyes to see.

Describe your relationship to Easter.

What does resurrection mean for you personally in your own life?

Easter Reflections 20__

Easter Reflections 20__

Easter Reflections 20__

Easter Reflections 20__

Easter Reflections 20___

Easter Reflections 20___

Easter Reflections 20___

Easter Reflections 20__

Easter Reflections 20__

The
Season
of
Pentecost

Golden Rain by Daniel Bonnell

Pentecost

"On the day of Pentecost, all the believers were meeting together in one place. Suddenly, there was a sound from heaven like the roaring of a mighty windstorm, and it filled the house where they were sitting. Then, what looked like flames or tongues of fire appeared and settled on each of them. And everyone present was filled with the Holy Spirit and began speaking in other languages, as the Holy Spirit gave them this ability."

Acts 2:1-4 NLT

"They were praising God as they were given affection before all the people, and Our Lord was adding unto the church every day those who were coming to life."

Acts 2:47 ABPE

Pentecost is one of the most ancient celebrations of the Church and is considered by Christians to be the day of its birth and the beginning of its witness to the nations of the world. Determined by the date of Easter, Pentecost is a moveable feast observed at the conclusion of Eastertide on the seventh Sunday after Easter. Consequently, Pentecost can occur as early as May 10 and as late as June 13. Also called Whitsunday by the English, in reference to the white robes worn by those new converts who were to be baptized on that day, the word "Pentecost" is actually a transliteration of the Greek word, pentekostos, which means "fifty." Originally, Pentecost was an ancient Jewish holy day of Thanksgiving celebrated fifty days after the beginning of the harvest. In time, Pentecost came to be a commemoration of God's giving of the Law to Moses at Mt. Sinai and was celebrated fifty days after the Feast of Passover. It was during the Jewish celebration of Pentecost, exactly fifty days after the Resurrection of Christ, that this day became of particular significance to believers in Christ. The second chapter of the New Testament book of *Acts* records this first century Pentecost event when the Holy Spirit came like a strong wind and descended upon the first followers of Jesus. God's promise to pour-out His Spirit upon all flesh bore witness with this empowerment, evidenced by "tongues of fire" and the gift to speak in other languages, as the disciples boldly proclaimed Christ to the world. The Church uses the color red for sanctuary adornments on Pentecost Sunday. It symbolizes both the tongues of fire as well as the fire of the Holy Spirit kindled in the followers of Christ to spread the Gospel. Many of the thousands present in Jerusalem that day were amazed to hear the telling of the *Good News* of salvation for all mankind in their own languages. Those who heard the divine message and believed with gladness the witness of the disciples about the love of God in Christ, repented from their sins and were baptized, so that about 3,000 were added to the Church on that day. Thanks be to God that the Risen Christ still comes in the same unique and personal way, imparting new life to each person who opens his heart to receive His love, forgiveness and the indwelling Presence of the Holy Spirit.

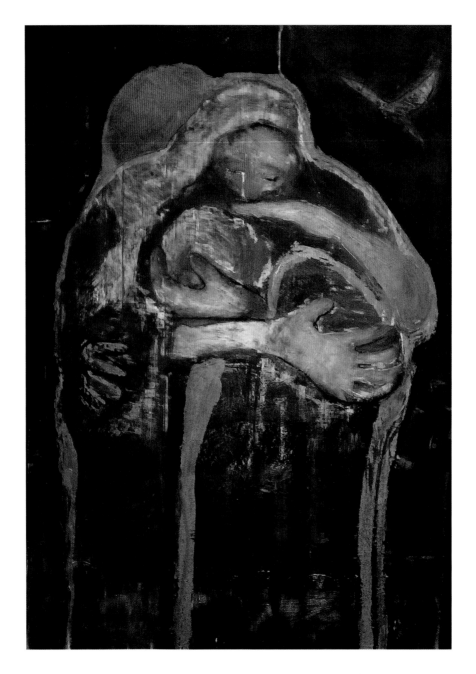

The Father's Forgiveness by Daniel Bonnell

96

The Wishing Well
Adapted from Padraic Pearse's, *Renunciation* by Connie Dover
Additional verses by Lana Lee Marler

When first I saw You,
I saw beauty,
And I blinded my eyes
For fear that I should weep.

When first I heard You,
I heard sweetness,
And I turned away
For fear of my weakness.

I blinded my eyes,
My face I turned away;
I hardened my heart
For fear of my ruin.

But Your love, my Lord
I cannot forsake;
Silent tears wash my soul,
A vow I would make.

I opened my eyes;
My face turned not away.
Purest joy fills my heart;
I rest in Your embrace.

Reflection on "The Wishing Well"
by Roger Housden

This poem echoes a much older one by the 17th century English poet, George Herbert - which goes to show us how the sentiments expressed are intrinsic to the human experience, and have been so for all time. Herbert's poem is called "Love," and I think it is worth citing here in its entirety.

Love bade me welcome; yet my soul drew back,
        Guilty of dust and sin.
But quick-eyed Love, observing me grow slack
        From my first entrance in,
Drew nearer to me, sweetly questioning
        If I lack'd anything.

'A guest,' I answer'd, 'worthy to be here:'
        Love said, 'You shall be he.'
'I, the unkind, ungrateful? Ah, my dear,
        I cannot look on Thee.'
Love took my hand and smiling did reply,
        'Who made the eyes but I?'

'Truth, Lord; but I have marr'd them: Let my shame
        Go where it doth deserve.'
'And know you not,' says Love, 'Who bore the blame?'
        'My dear, then I will serve.'
'You must sit down,' says Love, 'and taste my meat.'
        So I did sit and eat.

Have you ever felt like the person in either of these two poems? That you are unworthy of God's love? Write your response to one or both of these poems.

Pentecost Reflections 20__

Pentecost Reflections 20__

Pentecost Reflections 20___

Pentecost Reflections 20__

Pentecost Reflections 20__

Pentecost Reflections 20__

Pentecost Reflections 20__

Pentecost Reflections 20___

Pentecost Reflections 20__

The
Season of
Ordinary
Time

The Good Shepherd by Daniel Bonnell

Ordinary Time

"Now when Jesus came into the district of Caesare'a Philip'pi, he asked his disciples, 'Who do men say that the Son of man is?' And they said, 'Some say John the Baptist, others say Eli'jah, and others Jeremiah or one of the prophets.' He said to them, 'But who do you say that I am?' Simon Peter replied, 'You are the Christ, the Son of the living God.' And Jesus answered him, 'Blessed are you, Simon Bar-Jona! For flesh and blood has not revealed this to you, but my Father who is in heaven. And I tell you, you are Peter, and on this rock I will build my church, and the powers of death shall not prevail against it. I will give you the keys of the kingdom of heaven, and whatever you bind on earth shall be bound in heaven, and whatever you loose on earth shall be loosed in heaven.'" Matthew 16:13-19 RSV

The Seasons of Advent, Christmas, Epiphany, Lent, Easter and Pentecost are the Liturgical Seasons around which the movement of sacred time is organized within the church calendar year. The succession of weeks occurring outside the major festivals in the liturgical calendar, specifically after Epiphany and Pentecost, is known as "Ordinary Time." First introduced at the Second Vatican Council (1962-65), this season of the newly-reformed Roman liturgical calendar was not coined to relegate this period of time to a lesser status, as the term "ordinary" might imply. The English word "ordinary" is derived from the Latin word "ordo," meaning numbers in a series. Thus, whether in the Roman or Protestant tradition, "Ordinary Time" is called "ordinary" because it is counted time. The two periods of successively numbered weeks after Epiphany on Jan. 6th, until the day before the beginning of Lent, and then, after Pentecost Sunday until the day before Advent, constitute "Ordinary Time." Rather than feasting or penance fundamental to the major seasons of the church year, "Ordinary Time" is a period devoted to the contemplation of the mystery of Christ in all its aspects, including His imminent return. Although churches may introduce a variety of colors to distinguish this season from the "ordinary," the color green has traditionally been associated with growth and rebirth and is most often used to adorn the church Sanctuary or *Nave* during "Ordinary Time." Encouraging growth for its members during this season, the Church focuses on the application of scripture readings from one of the annual Synoptic Gospels and the mission of the Church to proclaim Christ to the world for the transformation of lives. At the conclusion of the "Ordinary Time" season, the cycle of the Liturgical Calendar returns to its beginning with the "Advent" of a new year. Therefore, it is fitting that our response to the Gospel message during this season should be for our souls to long to return to a renewed relationship with God.

Glimpse of an Angel by Daniel Bonnell

Back to the Garden

by

Lana Lee Marler

I long to see myself in a knowing sky;
And be wrapped in warm colors as down I lie.
Then closing my eyes, find rest in the beauty
Of the Love Song that has ever called to me.

O sing me to sleep and sing me awake,
And sing me alive because my soul aches
To give my whole self to the Music within,
Calling me back to the Garden again.

There are holes in my soul that trouble me.
Holes blocking out light
And then letting none leave;
Darkening portals of loathing and fear,
These holes through which I cannot see or hear.

My soul's dark cradle is stirred in the night
By shimmering echoes of belonging and light;
Summoning yearnings for deep harmony
With all things present or coming to be.

O sing me to sleep and sing me awake,
And sing me alive because my soul aches
To give my whole self to the Music within,
Calling me back to the Garden again.

The Garden of Peace where by Love was first held;
The Garden of Peace where Love holds me still.

Reflection on "Back to the Garden"
by Roger Housden

The apostle Peter is a very appropriate figure to identify with a season of ordinary time. For all his enthusiasm and vigor, and even though he recognized Jesus for who he was immediately, and left everything to follow him, Peter was also the first to betray Jesus. He shows us his fear on more than one occasion, and throughout the Gospels he is portrayed as the most human of the disciples, with as much darkness in him as light. Peter is all of us. He knows the Garden, that place beyond space and time of perfect peace and beatitude; and he knows that the music of that garden is inside him. Yet he also knows that there are dark places in his soul that block out the light, and he cries out for the Holy Spirit to take him to that Garden of Peace where Love holds him still.

Has some similar prayer ever left your own lips?

Ordinary Time Reflections 20__

Ordinary Time Reflections 20__

Ordinary Time Reflections 20__

Ordinary Time Reflections 20__

Ordinary Time Reflections 20__

Ordinary Time Reflections 20__

Ordinary Time Reflections 20__

Ordinary Time Reflections 20__

Ordinary Time Reflections 20__

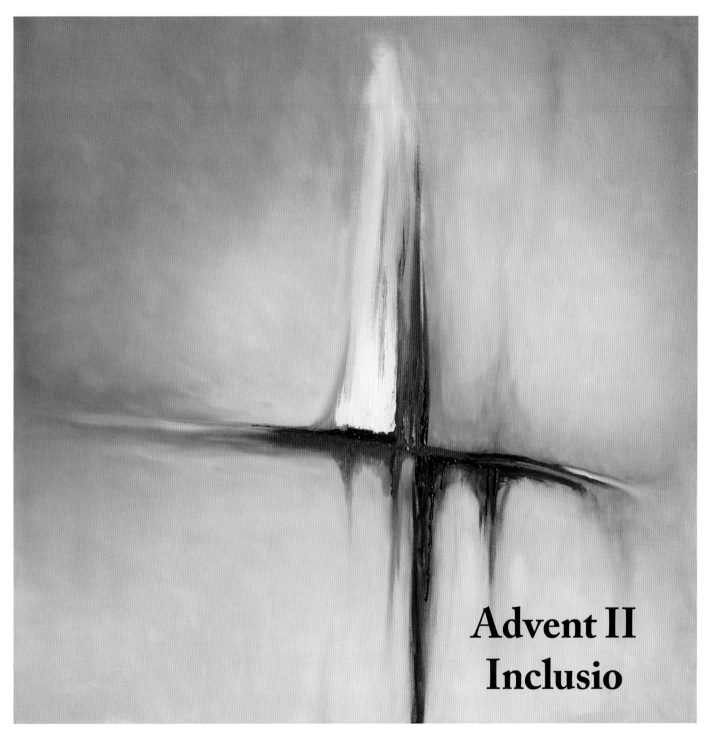

**Advent II
Inclusio**

Let the Children Come by Daniel Bonnell

Advent II

"For since we believe that Jesus died and rose again, even so, through Jesus, God will bring with him those who have died. For this we declare to you by the word of the Lord, that we who are alive, who are left until the coming of the Lord, will by no means precede those who have died. For the Lord himself, with a cry of command, with the archangel's call and with the sound of God's trumpet, will descend from heaven, and the dead in Christ will rise first. Then we who are alive, who are left, will be caught up in the clouds together with them to meet the Lord in the air; and so we will be with the Lord forever." I Thessalonians 4:14-17 NRSV

Most Christians in the traditional Church understand the English word, Advent, which is derived from the Latin, *adventus*, meaning "coming" or "arrival," as it relates to the Coming of Christ into the world at His birth. However, this same word, translated *parousia* in New Testament Greek, is also commonly used in reference to the Second Coming of Christ. The Advent of Christ has been a basic theme of creedal statements in the traditional church whereby Christians affirm that Christ has come; Christ has died; Christ is risen; and Christ will come again. The Nicene Creed, the ancient creed or profession of faith most widely used in Christian liturgy, likewise includes apocalyptic language: "He (Jesus Christ) ascended into heaven and is seated at the right hand of the Father. He will come again in glory to judge the living and the dead and His kingdom will have no end." Consequently, during the Season of Advent each year in the Liturgical Calendar, there is a dual emphasis on past and future – the commemoration of the birth of Christ the Savior in His First Advent and the anticipation of the return of Christ the King in His Second Advent.

In Western Christianity, purple is the traditional color used for clergy vestments and hangings to adorn the Sanctuary during Advent, but the practice of replacing purple with blue to denote a hopeful attitude of awe and anticipation has gained popularity in recent years. The lighting of candles is also an important symbol for each of the four Sundays in this liturgical season. The first candle to be lighted is traditionally the Candle of Expectation or Hope. Because we live in a world that is not yet fully reconciled to God, we await the Second Advent of Christ with the same hope and expectation as did the ancient world in His First Advent.

The Apostle Paul refers to the Second Advent of the Lord as "that blessed hope" (Titus 2:13) and "the hope of eternal life...which is laid up for you in heaven (Titus 1:2; Col. 1:5). In I Peter, we are reminded that God "has begotten us again unto a lively hope by the resurrection of Jesus Christ from the dead, to an inheritance incorruptible, and undefiled, and that fades not away, reserved in heaven for you . . . salvation ready to be revealed in the last time." (1 Pet. 1:35)

The Advent scripture readings have a dual emphasis on both "Comings" of Christ, including themes of preparedness, faithfulness, judgment of sin and eternal life. The twin themes of Advent are aptly illustrated in the parable of the bridesmaids who anxiously wait for the coming of the Bridegroom. (Matt 25:1-13) While there is intense joy in the anticipation of the Bridegroom's coming, there is more than an implied warning for the need to prepare for His return. Stern admonishments notwithstanding, it is the transcendent nature of the hope requisite to the triumphant Parousia of Christ/ Advent II as described by the Apostle Paul, which has served to captivate the hearts and minds of believers over the centuries: "For the Lord himself shall descend from heaven with a shout, with the voice of the archangel, and with the trump of God: and the dead in Christ shall rise first: Then we which are alive and remain shall be caught up together with them in the clouds, to meet the Lord in the air: and so shall we ever be with the Lord." (I Thessalonians 4:16-17) And since no one but the Father knows the hour when Christ will return (Matt. 24:36); He could come *any day now...*

One bright
morning when
this life
is over...

I'll fly away.

I'll Fly Away by Daniel Bonnell

Any Day Now

by

Lana Lee Marler

Any day now, my heart will hear God say,
"Now is the time, My Son is on the way."
This bird loosed from its cage, no more to roam;
Any day now, my God will call me home.

Any day now,
Changed in the twinkling of an eye,
At the trump sound and to my glad surprise;
Then the love beams will fall
From heaven to the ground.
Any day now, I will not be around.

Loved ones, He's coming soon, our Savior,
And we shall meet Him in the air;
To live and sing His praise until forever.
No more holding on to this life as before.

Any day now, with all those called by His name;
Quickly I'll rise, there's no more tears or pain;
This bird loosed from its cage, no more to roam.
Any day now, God's love will bid me, "Come!"

Loved ones, He's coming soon, our Savior;
And we shall meet Him in the air;
To live and sing His praise until forever.
No more holding on to this life as before.

Then the love beams will fall
From heaven to the ground;
And we shall meet Him in the air;
To live and sing His praise
Until forever.
Any day now; Any day now...
We're heaven bound.

Reflection on "Any Day Now"
by Roger Housden

Could it be possible that the day you may be wishing for is the very one you are living now? We are so accustomed to living in the past or the future - so used to hoping that something wonderful is going to happen tomorrow - that we can all too easily forget the miracle we are living at this very moment. If we stop and still ourselves for a moment, we may feel in our bones and not just in our mind that we really do not know what this Extraordinary life is. The intuition that the majesty of the spirit can burst into our day at any moment can fill us with awe and even dread. The poet, Emily Dickinson, reminds us that "the soul should always stand ajar ready to welcome the ecstatic experience." Can you imagine the Second Coming as a deep interior experience? What might that feel like? What would it mean?

If you prefer to see it as an external world event, describe your faith in that and how it contributes to your present life.

Advent II Reflections 20__

Advent II Reflections 20__

Advent II Reflections 20__

Advent II Reflections 20___

Advent II Reflections 20___

Advent II Reflections 20___

Advent ‖ Reflections 20__

Advent II Reflections 20__

Advent II Reflections 20___

Works Cited

From the CD, *The Wishing Well*, Words adapted from *Renunciation* by Padraic Pearse [1916] Public Domain by Connie Dover © 1994 Taylor Park Music, Inc. Used by permission.

Love (III), Public Domain [1632] George Herbert.

Quotation from *Prayers of Life* by Michel Quoist is reproduced courtesy of Gill and Macmillan Ltd. 1965.

Scriptures marked KJV are taken from the KING JAMES VERSION (KJV): KING JAMES VERSION is Public Domain in the United States.

Scriptures marked NIV are taken from THE HOLY BIBLE, NEW INTERNATIONAL VERSION®, NIV® Copyright © 1973, 1978, 1984, 2011 by Biblica, Inc.® Used by permission. All rights reserved worldwide.

Scriptures marked RSV are taken from the REVISED STANDARD VERSION of the Bible copyright ©1946, 1952, and 1971 the Division of Christian Education of the National Council of the Churches of Christ in the United States of America. Used by permission. All rights reserved.

Scriptures marked NLT are taken from the HOLY BIBLE, NEW LIVING TRANSLATION copyright © 1996, 2004, 2007 by Tyndale House Foundation. Used by permission of Tyndale House Publishers, Inc., Carol Stream, Illinois 60188. All rights reserved.

Scriptures marked NRSV are taken from the NEW REVISED STANDARD VERSION Bible, copyright © 1989, the Division of Christian Education of the National Council of

Artists

My painting reflects on the ultimate human need to fulfill an intrinsic longing that extends from birth to death. Simply put, it is a need to be held. My art symbolically speaks to this notion, especially with darkness (black) embracing light (color), with negative space enclosing positive space, and with texture calling out to be touched. I paint primarily on grocery bag paper with mis-tinted house paint. In my process this surface is surrogate for human skin that reflects life, especially so, when the heavy paper is saturated with pigments, oils, wax, and fragrances. The concept of using something that was once a utilitarian container also speaks to the theme of being held. My latest paintings follow a path wherein they are recycled back into yet another painting, as if it were sacrificing itself for a greater work. The painting is never finished, it is only at rest. Such a process is known as kenosis, or purging of the essence within each painting to create a greater work of art. This process is born out of contemplative thought and writings of the mystics. Working on modest surfaces with humble means permits this direction in a very natural manner. My paintings become a creative conductor that allows me to be held.

--Daniel Bonnell

Roy Borrone works in the tradition of gestural painting, where ideas grow out of the very act of painting itself. Long investments such as these create a language that carries a relevance to ideas, a quality that is missing in other work today. Roy is an incredible artist who believes more in the development of his vision than in the production of acceptable objects.

--Nathan Oliveira

Mike Irwin of Dallas, Texas was trained in art since childhood and has years of experience painting abstract works on canvas. He spends his free time pursuing additional creative ventures as a musician, photographer, and graphic artist. Mike has enjoyed his creative journey and is motivated by the idea that he may have only just scratched the surface of what his artistic future holds. See Mike's current portfolio at www.mikeirwinart.com.

Narrators

Rev. William D. Marler, a United Methodist minister and Executive Director of Jacob's Ladder Community Development Corporation served as the main narrator for the audio book. By happy coincidence, he is also the spouse of the author of *Follow Me - A Seasonal Journey*.

Leslie Cromwell, lead project consultant and co-owner of Lamplight Studio, narrated the Preface and Introduction of the audio book.

Featured Music Arranger

Jeremey Johnson, American composer and arranger, has been writing music in a variety of settings for more than fourteen years. He studied music at Ball State University followed by Indiana Wesleyan University. Including a degree in music education, Jeremey has a vast spectrum of experience from many genres that drives the creativity of his distinctly unique style, which has become a hallmark of new music in many circles. He is also a sought after clinician and conductor throughout the country. As owner and founder of High Note Music Industries, Jeremey provides of number of music services to both professionals and amateurs worldwide.

Sound Engineers

Music recorded by Daniel Lynn, House Engineer and Manager of Music & Arts Studio in Memphis, TN. He has worked on projects ranging from local albums to world-wide film releases. A self-proclaimed audio nerd, he loves achieving a true analogue sound using tape and other pieces of outboard gear.

Vocals and narration engineered by Mark Polack at Lamplight Studio, owned by Leslie and Chad Cromwell, on Lamplight Farms outside of Nashville, TN.

Music editing, mixing, mastering and also produced by Mark Polack at Knob Hill Studio. Mark is a mix engineer, tracking engineer, session bass player, programmer and songwriter based in Nashville, TN. He has worked with such greats: as Kenny Loggins, Richard Marx, Paul Carrack (Squeeze, Mike & the Mechanics), John Oates (Hall & Oates), Tommy Sims (Bruce Springsteen, Bonnie Raitt, Sheryl Crow), Reggie Young (Elvis Presley, Waylon Jennings, Johnny Cash). Tom Petersson (Cheap Trick), Felix Cavaliere (the Rascals), producer Peter Collins (Rush, Elton John, Indigo Girls), Jewel, and Kellie Pickler, to name a few. He also worked on the Time Life/Waylon Jennings Project, *Goin' Down Rockin'*.

Music mastering by Richard Dodd, a mastering engineer, mix engineer and producer based in Nashville, TN. He has worked with such artists as Tom Petty And The Heartbreakers, Delbert McClinton, George Harrison, Roy Orbison, Boz Scaggs, Wilco, Green Day, Steve Earle, Robert Plant and The Traveling Wilburys to name a few.

Music

The Longing
Lyrics and Music by Lana Lee Marler, arr. Jeremey Johnson; Violin - Mariama Alcantara; Flute - Aaron Boquet; Oboe - Drew Spencer-Bell; Cello 1 - Diego Rodriquez; Cello 2 - Anto Rodriquez; Vocal - Lana Lee Marler

Even So, Come
Lyrics and Music by Lana Lee Marler; Piano - Owen Brophy, Vocal - Lana Lee Marler

Epiphany
Lyrics and Music by Lana Lee Marler; Piano - Owen Brophy, Vocal - Lana Lee Marler

Surrender
Lyrics by Lana Lee Marler, arr. Lana Lee Marler and Jeremey Johnson; Flute - DeLara Hashemi; Clarinet in B flat - Amelia Smith; Oboe - Drew Spencer-Bell; Horn in F - George Hranov; Bassoon - Nicole Neeley; Vocal - Lana Lee Marler

The Beauty of Your Love
Lyrics by Lana Lee Marler, arr. Lana Lee Marler and Jeremey Johnson; Violin 1 – Mariama Alcantara; Violin 2 - Hannah Hart; Viola - Molly Wilkens-Reed; Horn in F - George Hranov; Cello - Diego Rodriquez; Double Bass - Andrew Knote; Vocal - Lana Lee Marler

The Wishing Well
Original Lyrics and Music by Connie Dover, additional lyrics and arr. by Lana Lee Marler; Piano-Owen Brophy; Synthesized Strings - Owen Brophy; Penny Whistle 1 - Jeanne Simmons; Penny Whistle 2 - Jeanne Simmons; Vocal - Lana Lee Marler

Back to the Garden
Lyrics and Music by Lana Lee Marler, arr. Jeremey Johnson; Penny Whistle 1 - Jeanne Simmons; Penny Whistle 2 - Jeanne Simmons; Cello - Diego Rodriquez; Vocal - Lana Lee Marler

Any Day Now
Lyrics by Lana Lee Marler, arr. Lana Lee Marler and Jeremey Johnson; Piano and Synthesized Strings - Owen Brophy; Flute - Aaron Boquet; Oboe - Drew Spencer-Bell; Vocal - Lana Lee Marler

Contributing Writer

ROGER HOUSDEN is the author of twenty books on poetry, art and pilgrimage, including the best-selling Ten Poems to Change Your Life series, and the anthology *For Lovers of God Everywhere: Poems of the Christian Mystics*. He uses writing as a teaching tool for personal exploration and reflection, and runs regular courses around the country, including Bishop's Ranch, the Episcopalian Retreat center in Sonoma. He is a well-known presenter and speaker for Unity churches and radio. His latest book, *Keeping The Faith Without a Religion*, was published on March 1, 2014 with Sounds True. You can book him as a speaker/workshop leader and also see his current live and online courses at www.rogerhousden.com. You can also sign up for his mailing list on his home page and receive a weekly poem with Roger's reflections.

About the Author

LANA LEE MARLER is a poet, singer/song writer, and church music director. A wife and mother, she is also a partner in ministry with her husband who is a United Methodist minister. Lana is an artist in any medium, but long ago chose music to express her relationship to God. Her faith journey led her to a major in sacred music in college and has crossed the landscape of three denominations: Baptist, Methodist and Episcopal. Spending countless hours mastering the hymnody and liturgies of these quite varied traditions has added depth and richness to her Christian perspective. Moreover, her musical DNA is infused with the music of the times in which she grew-up - the 1960's. Whether the song is Joan Baez's "Swing Low" or "Just As I Am" sung from a back row Baptist pew, she connects with each tradition in authenticity. In 2004, Lana and her husband, Rev. William D. Marler, co-founded Jacob's Ladder™ Community Development Corporation, a non-profit charity serving inner-city Memphis, where the Gospel of Christ is shared through community-building, home rehabilitation and education (jacobsladdercdc.org). All proceeds from this book will go to benefit the community served by Jacob's Ladder™.